Weekly Reader Books presents

Saying What You Mean

A Children's Book about Communication Skills

by

Joy Wilt

Illustrated by Ernie Hergenroeder

Educational Products Division

Word, Incorporated

Waco, Texas

Author

JOY WILT is creator and director of Children's Ministries, an organization that provides resources "for people who care about children"—speakers, workshops, demonstrations, consulting services, and training institutes. A certified elementary school teacher, administrator, and early childhood specialist, Joy is also consultant to and professor in the master's degree program in children's ministries for Fuller Theological Seminary. Joy is a graduate of LaVerne College, LaVerne, California (B.A. in Biological Science), and Pacific Oaks College, Pasadena, California (M.A. in Human Development). She is author of three books, *Happily Ever After, An Uncomplicated Guide to Becoming a Superparent,* and *Taming the Big Bad Wolves,* as well as the popular *Can-Make-And-Do Books.* Joy's commitment "never to forget what it feels like to be a child" permeates the many innovative programs she has developed and her work as lecturer, consultant, writer, and—not least—mother of two children, Christopher and Lisa.

Artist

ERNIE HERGENROEDER is founder and owner of Hergie & Associates (a visual communications studio and advertising agency). With the establishment of this company in 1975, "Hergie" and his wife, Faith, settled in San Jose with their four children, Lynn, Kathy, Stephen, and Beth. Active in community and church affairs, Hergie is involved in presenting creative workshops for teachers, ministers, and others who wish to understand the techniques of communicating visually. He also lectures in high schools to encourage young artists toward a career in commercial art. Hergie serves as a consultant to organizations such as the Police Athletic League (PAL), Girl Scouts, and religious and secular corporations. His ultimate goal is to touch the hearts of kids (8 to 80) all over the world—visually!

This book is a presentation of Weekly Reader Books.
Weekly Reader Books offers book clubs for children from
preschool through junior high school.

For further information write to:
WEEKLY READER BOOKS
1250 Fairwood Ave.
Columbus, Ohio 43216

Saying What You Mean

7 8 9 / 86 85

Contents

Introduction

Saying What You Mean is one of a series of books. The complete set is called **Ready-Set-Grow!**

Saying What You Mean deals with communication skills and can be used by itself or as a part of a program that utilizes all of the **Ready-Set-Grow!** books.

Saying What You Mean is specifically designed for children four to eight years of age. A child can either read the book or have it read to him or her. This can be done at home, church, or school.

Saying What You Mean is designed to involve the child in the concepts that are being taught. This is done by simply and carefully explaining each concept and then asking questions that invite a response from the child. It is hoped that by answering the questions the child will personalize the concept and, thus, integrate it into his or her thinking.

Many problems and conflicts that arise in human relationships can be attributed to a "lack of communication." Poor communication often results from not understanding what communication is. For this reason, Saying What You Mean carefully defines and explains both verbal and nonverbal communication.

Saying What You Mean also strives to teach children how to communicate effectively. It teaches them that what one says will best be communicated when it is said at the right time to the right people in the right way. Saying What You Mean clearly outlines what constitutes the "right time," the "right people," and the "right way" so that children can begin to control what they say and how it is received.

You are a communicator.

You began being a communicator when you were a baby.

When you were hungry, you cried. Your cry communicated that you wanted something to eat.

When you were tired, you yawned and rubbed your eyes. Your yawn and sleepy eyes communicated that you needed to sleep.

When you were uncomfortable or frustrated, you
fussed and whined. Your fussing and whining
communicated that you needed help and attention.

13

When you were happy and content, you smiled, giggled, and cooed.

Your smiling, giggling, and cooing communicated that you liked whatever was happening and the way everything was at that moment.

14

Although you did not say any words, you communicated. From the very beginning of your life, you were a communicator.

Communication is exchanging or passing along feelings, thoughts, or information.

A communicator is one who exchanges or passes
along feelings, thoughts, or information.

You are a communicator.
You communicate every day with everyone around you.
You communicate in many ways.

Chapter 1

Communicating with Your Body

Sometimes you use your head to communicate. . .

"Yes."

"No."

Sometimes you use your face to communicate. . .

"I'm happy."

"I'm sad."

Your face can communicate. . .

"I'm mad."

"I'm annoyed and frustrated."

Your face can communicate. . .

"I'm thinking."

"I'm confused."

Your face can communicate. . .

"I'm surprised!"

"I'm worried."

Your face can communicate. . .

"I'm scared."

"I'm disappointed."

Sometimes you use your hands to say. . .

"No."

"OK."

Your hands can say. . .

"I hope so."

"Two."

Your hands can say. . .

"Shhh. That's too loud."

"I can't hear."

Sometimes you use your arms and hands to communicate...

"Hello and good-bye."

"Over there."

Your arms and hands can say. . .

"You."

"Me."

Your arms and hands can say. . .

"Give it to me."

"Take it."

Your arms and hands can say...

"Come here."

"Stay away."

Your arms and hands can say. . .

"I don't know."

"I won!"

Your arms and hands can say. . .

"You did a good job! I liked what you did!"

"Let's be friends."

Sometimes your whole body can communicate. . .

"I love you."

"I hate you."

Your body can say. . .

"I'm shy. Leave me alone."

"I feel rejected and alone."

Your body can say. . .

"I'm confident. I know I can do it."

"I'm proud of myself. I like the things I do."

You are a communicator.
You communicate every day with everyone around you.

You use your

head,
face,
hands,
arms,

and whole body to communicate.

Chapter 2

Communicating with Art, Music, Dance, Writing, and Drama

Sometimes you communicate through art.

Sometimes you communicate through music.

Sometimes you communicate
by dancing.

62

Sometimes you communicate by writing.

Sometimes you communicate through drama.

67

You are a communicator.
You communicate every day with everyone around you.

You can communicate through:

    art,
    music,
    dance,
    writing, or
    drama.

Chapter 3

Communicating with Words

Talking is another way you communicate.

When you talk, you use words.

Sometimes you need only one word to communicate.

Words like hello
yes
no
stop
go
wait
O K
look
please
thanks
sorry, and
don't   . . . are sometimes all you need
to communicate everything
you want to communicate.

At other times, you need more than one word to communicate.

Words are only letters of the alphabet put together.

What you do with words, how you put them together and how you say them, makes them a form of communication.

What you do with Words . . . .

The same words can communicate different messages.

The meaning you give to words depends upon many
things, such as. . .

I THINK YOU'RE THE MOST BEAUTIFUL GIRL I'VE EVER SEEN.

OH, STOP IT. YOU'RE EMBARRASSING ME.

how softly or. . .

how loudly you say them.

how fast you say them.

The meaning you give to words depends upon. . .

how unkindly you say them.

83

85

The meaning you give to words depends upon. . .

how enthusiastically or . . .

how unenthusiastically you say them.

The meaning you give to words depends upon. . .

what you are doing. . .

91

You are a communicator.
You communicate every day with everyone around you.
You can communicate by saying words:

softly or loudly,
slow or fast,
kindly or unkindly,
sincerely or insincerely,
confidently or timidly,
enthusiastically or unenthusiastically.

You can communicate by reinforcing the words you
say with what you do.

Chapter 4

Communicating What You Want to Communicate

(Saying What You Mean)

Sometimes you want to communicate to someone how you feel.

Sometimes you want to communicate to someone what you think.

Sometimes you want to communicate to someone what you want.

Sometimes you want to communicate to someone what you need.

97

Sometimes you want to communicate to someone
your hopes and dreams.

Sometimes you want to communicate to someone facts and information.

If you want to communicate important things like

   how you feel,
   what you think,
   what you want,
   what you need,
   your hopes and dreams,   or
   facts and information,

            . . . you need to do several things.

To begin with, important things need to be communicated at the right time.

It is not the right time to communicate important things. . .

if the person you want to communicate with is
too busy to think about what you are saying.

103

You need to wait for a time when you can communicate.

MOM, I'M NOT BUSY NOW. CAN YOU TALK?

You need to wait for a time when the person you
want to communicate with can listen, and then. . .

Communicate!

Second, important things need to be communicated to the right people.

People who are not interested in you are not the
right people to whom you should communicate
important things.

People who are not interested in what you are saying are not the right people to whom you should communicate important things.

You need to find someone who is interested in you.

You need to find someone who is interested in what you have to say, and then. . .

Communicate!

Third, important things need to be communicated
accurately and honestly.

is accurate and honest.

This boy's communication is not accurate and honest.

115

is accurate and honest.

This girl's communication is not accurate **?** and honest.

This boy's communication. . .

is accurate and honest.

This boy's communication is not accurate and honest.

Only when you communicate accurately and honestly can people know and understand what you want them to know and understand. Only when you communicate accurately and honestly can people respond accurately and honestly to you.

Before you communicate,
think about what you are going to say.

Then, say it as accurately

You are a communicator.
You communicate every day with everyone around you.
When you communicate important things, remember to:

communicate at the right time,
communicate to the right people, and
communicate accurately and honestly.

Conclusion

Good communication will help you get along
with other people. It can make your life happier.

Good communication all depends on how well you. . .

Say what you mean.